WOLFE TONE

First published in 2001 by Mercier Press
5 French Church St Cork
Tel: (021) 275040; Fax: (021) 274969; e.mail: books@mercier.ie
16 Hume Street Dublin 2
Tel: (01) 661 5299; Fax: (01) 661 8583; e.mail: books@marino.ie

Trade enquiries to CMD Distribution 55A Spruce Avenue
Stillorgan Industrial Park Blackrock County Dublin
Tel: (01) 294 2556; Fax: (01) 294 2564
e.mail: cmd@columba.ie

© Sean McMahon 2001
A CIP record for this book is available from the British Library.

ISBN 1 85635 339 7
10 9 8 7 6 5 4 3 2 1

Cover design by Penhouse Design
Printed in Ireland by ColourBooks Baldoyle Dublin 13

WOLFE TONE

SEAN McMAHON

MERCIER PRESS

CONTENTS

CHRONOLOGY

1792	Appointed agent to the Catholic Committee; Catholics allowed to practice law
1793	Ceases to act as agent when committee dissolves itself; Catholic Relief Act removes much of the residual penal legislation and grants the same county voting rights to Catholics as Protestants enjoyed
1795	After involvement in Jackson affair, leaves for USA with family; Orange Order formed in County Armagh
1796	Arrives in France and succeeds in arranging a French invasion fleet, which is unable to land in Bantry Bay because of bad weather
1797	Dutch invasion fleet unable to sail because of adverse winds; later annihilated at Camperdown; Tone united with family in Hamburg; meets Napoleon to discuss yet another invasion of Ireland; General Lake imposes a form of martial law in Ulster
1798	Risings in the Pale, Antrim, Down, Wexford and Mayo; Tone arrested when the *Hoche,* as flagship of yet another invasion force, surrenders after a six-hour naval battle in Lough Swilly; taken ashore in Buncrana, County Donegal; sentenced to death; dies from self-inflicted wound on 19 November

1

THE COACHBUILDER'S SON

The Ireland into which Theobald Wolfe Tone was born on 20 June 1763 was still, in terms of administration, land-owning and the personnel of a majority of professions, essentially a Protestant nation. The majority Catholic population – something under 4 million, compared with just under 1 million Protestants – was precluded by stringent anti-popery laws from owning land, holding service commissions or any office of state, practising law, becoming members of Parliament or even voting. The anti-clerical laws, however, were not universally enforced, and there was a toleration of low-level practice of religion; even bishops, who had been specifically expelled by the Bishops' Banishment Act of 1697, were, with proper lack of ostentation, permitted to rule dioceses in which clergy in mufti administered the sacraments and held divine services in 'chapels'. The Penal Laws, as later generations termed them, were copies of legislation that was on the statute books of Westminster, but, apart from the activities of local zealots, serious interference with the practice of Catholicism was uncommon. There was no desire that this subject majority should be converted to Protestantism; it was sufficient that they were quiescent.

Though prevented from taking part in public life and the more refined professions, there was no bar on entrepreneurial Catholics becoming successful in trade. For one thing, the occupation was held in contempt by the Ascendancy, with the sons of some rising Protestant merchants, when they could, energetically sloughing off the metaphorical apron for the silk gown of the advocate. For the families of the residual Catholic aristocracy, commerce provided an appropriate career for third sons – the first and second often having careers in foreign armies and the Church. The long peace, too, had seen an increase in the population and, because of the somnolent state of agriculture, a drift to the towns. The in-

dustrious with business acumen soon rose above
the proletarian level and began to amass wealth.
Their social disadvantages meant that opportun-
ities for display and wasteful spending were
limited; many became very rich indeed, providing
their sons with a Continental education to
compensate for the penal deprivation at home
and consolidating their position independently
of land possession.

The result of minority disdain on the one
hand and earnest endeavour on the other was
that, especially in the cities and large towns, a
strong and rich Catholic merchant class existed
– and would not much longer bear its nullity in
the eyes of the state. The fears that Catholics
might – as during the Counter-Reformation
and the troubled seventeenth century – be
manipulated by Continental enemies of Britain
had proved groundless for fifty years. In spite of
the authorities' stated expectation, Catholics
had not responded in any significant way to
Charles Stuart's adventure in 1745, and they
had presented formal evidence of loyalty to the
new king at his accession in 1760. Their mien
during the recent war with France, which had

ended four months before Tone's birth, made it clear that the old bugbear of Jacobitism and Continental Catholic invasion had been exorcised. And this acquiescence in loyalty to the Crown was to continue during the American Revolutionary War (1775–83), when it was the Catholics who supported the British forces, while many Protestants vociferously favoured the colonists. (Many in Ulster had kinsfolk in Washington's armies.)

With such wealth at its disposal, the merchant class was bound eventually to demand social and political reform. Initial moves were low-key: a Catholic Association of Dublin businessmen had been founded in 1756 to seek better conditions for trade, and in 1760 Charles O'Conor (1710–91) of Belanagare, County Roscommon, an antiquarian landowner – who had had to buy off his Protestant younger brother, according to the current penal law of inheritance – John Curry (c. 1710–80), a doctor – a profession permitted to Catholics – and Thomas Wyse (c. 1700–70), a Waterford squire who also had a milling business, formed a Catholic Committee in 1760. The committee was far from homogeneous, the residual Catholic peers and the bishops finding little common ground with the bourgeois members. For many years it was riven by dissent and contented itself with mild reproaches and frequent statements of loyalty to a largely unheeding George III. Still, Relief Acts did follow, and by 1782 Catholics were able to buy property again and had had most of the education and religious prohibitions against them rescinded. Political expediency, rather than the committee's efforts, lay behind these ameliorations but some credit was taken by the still-uneasy alliance. It was, however, that same committee – but with a much more vigorous membership and a decidedly militant stance – that was to have the benefit of the bright young lawyer Tone as agent in 1792.

Tone's father, Peter, was a prosperous coach-builder with land in Bodenstown, County Kildare, and his mother, Margaret Lamport, was the Catholic daughter of a West Indian trader but became a Protestant in 1771. Tone was born at 27 St Bride's Street, near Dublin Castle, but the family soon moved north of the river, to 44 Stafford Street – which is now named after its most famous resident. The eldest of sixteen children, he soon proved a bright if lazy scholar, with the convenient capacity of being able to make up in a week or so the studies of a whole term. He was taken at age twelve, as noted in his *Memoirs,* from 'an excellent English school kept by Sisson Darling' to the Latin school of the Reverend William Craig:

> As the school was in the same street where we lived and as I was under my father's eye, I began Latin with ardour, and continued for a year or two with great diligence, when I began Greek, which I found still more to my taste.

His manifest destiny was a fellowship at Trinity but, though an abnormally quick study, he had great bouts of indolence and 'a regular system of what is called *mitching*', when he and his schoolfellows sampled the sights of the town and the nearby countryside, walking, swimming and viewing with dazzled eyes the 'parades, field days and reviews of the garrison in Dublin in the Phoenix Park'.

In 1778 Peter Tone, whose business was already in decline, was forced to sell up after injuries sustained in a fall. He went to live in the family property in Bodenstown, and Tone, at sixteen, had the freedom of city lodgings. His love of military trappings continued and, as a man who was naturally susceptible to women, he anticipated the effect 'that a red coat and cockade, with a pair of gold epaulettes' would have on the 'objects of his adoration'. A career in the army seemed more agreeable than academe and, but for the tardy intervention of Craig, Tone might have had an entirely different career. His teacher, realising that his pupil would not pass his entrance examination for college, informed his father of his son's military ambitions and his dereliction of his studies. For once, the tolerant father was adamant: the young Tone sat down 'with a very bad grace, to pull up my lost time; and at length, after labouring for some time sorely against the grain, I entered a pensioner of Trinity College in February 1781.' (Pensioners – those undergraduates who paid fees, but at the lowest level, £15 a year – made up the majority of the student body.)

The yearning for the military life never quite left him. The *Memoirs* were begun in Paris in August 1796 with the words:

> As I shall embark in a business within a few days, the event of which is uncertain, I take the opportunity of a vacant hour to throw on paper a few memorandums relative to myself and family, which may amuse the boys, for whom I write them, in case they should thereafter fall into their hands.

The 'business' was the sailing of a French invasion fleet to Bantry Bay and 'the few days' became four months. Yet he was clearly pleased to be able to write that 'the untameable desire which I have ever since had to become a soldier, a desire which has never once quit me, and which, after sixteen years of various adventures, I am at last at liberty to indulge.'

By now the nature of Tone's personality was becoming clear. He was talented, but reluctant to work steadily at subjects that did not interest him. Time and again he was rescued from the consequences of this sloth by a remarkable capacity for intense application. He was impulsive, witty, self-aware and very much of his class, knowing little of the mass of Irish Catholics and out of sympathy with the 'hidden Ireland' and the Gaelic tradition. His time in Trinity was undistinguished for so clever a student, though his capacity for intense if intermittent self-exertion was shown in his winning of a scholarship in 1784. The lure of the red coat and gold epaulettes struck again in 1783, when he 'returned with eagerness to my military plan' and wished to join the army and fight against the rebel Americans. Another stand-off with his sorely tried father resulted; the petulant Tone refused for the space of a year to open a book that did not deal with military matters; it meant the loss of a year. In fact, because of a number of inappropriate events, he did not graduate until 1786, when he was twenty-three. He narrowly missed expulsion, for example, because of his acting as second in a duel in which his principal was killed.

The most positive application of his time in Trinity was his membership of the Historical

Society, which had been founded by the great Edmund Burke (1729-97) in 1747. This was no mere Saturday-night debating society but an intensive course in adult education, with prizes offered for oratory and historical disquisition. Tone won medals for rhetoric, for which – with a harsh, thin, guttural voice – he was ill-equipped vocally, but his matter was always sound and carefully argued. He had discovered an ability in forensic and political writing which was to bring him public acclaim and would in time direct his mind to the action that was the logical sequel to his arguments. He became the society's auditor – the equivalent of president – in his final year. (One of his spiritual heirs, Thomas Davis (1814–45), was to use the same office in the same society fifty years later to adumbrate the principles of Young Ireland.)

The young man in his early twenties was not handsome: with a low forehead, pale, thin, pock-marked face and a rather long and prominent nose, he scarcely met the contemporary Belvederian standards of male beauty. Yet he was so lively and his conversation so witty that he captivated both men and women. Charles

Kendal Bushe (1767–1843) – who had been at school with Tone and was an undergraduate at Trinity at the same time as him, though he was four years younger than Tone, and was afterwards Lord Chief Justice – testified to his charm and defended him vigorously, in spite of his revolutionary career.

Two women, among admittedly several others ('one or two fugitive passions'), dominated Tone's undergraduate life. The first probably grew weary of his romantic but unphysical passion, since she was afterwards named by her husband in a criminal conversation case and was divorced by him. Tone got to know Eliza Martin through a shared interest in amateur dramatics. (Tom Moore, the minstrel boy, met his wife, Bessy Dyke, in similar circumstances, he playing Peeping Tom to her Lady Godiva in Kilkenny in 1809.) Eliza was the wife of the Connemara landowner later known as Humanity Dick (1754–1834) because of his founding of the RSPCA in 1824. She and Tone appeared as Lord and Lady Randolph in 'the celebrated tragedy of *Douglas*' and also in the farce *All the World's a Stage*, which was its curtain-raiser on 8 August 1783 in the little theatre that Eliza's husband had built in Kirwan's Lane.

The affair lasted for two years and completed Tone's *éducation sentimentale;* they parted after a row about swearing an affidavit. His regrets were soon assuaged when one evening in the spring of 1785 he saw a beautiful young girl sitting in a window in Grafton Street. She was Martha Witherington, the daughter of a woollen draper and sister of one of his acquaintances at Trinity. She was fifteen – and as smitten by the young man as he with her – when he used Edward Witherington to achieve entrée into her house. They eloped on 25 July and spent their honeymoon in Maynooth after being wed in St Ann's Church in Dawson Street. The couple remained happily married, Martha even agreeing to be renamed Matilda, after the character, a peerless wife and mother, played by Eliza Martin in *Douglas.* Relations with the Witheringtons, which were at first, not surprisingly, glacial, gradually improved, so that, when Tone returned to Dublin in 1788 to read for the bar, Martha's grandfather, the Reverend Mr Savage, made him a gift of £500 to enable

him to begin his law practice. He graduated
Bachelor of Laws in February 1789 and was
called to the Irish bar that summer.

2

THE LAW AND THE PAMPHLETS

Marriage rendered Tone ineligible for a fellow-ship at Trinity and, for a young man in need of a career, the law was the obvious option. Tone at this time was a young man in search of a career or, as he might have seen it, a role. The siren red coat and epaulettes still crooned, but by the spring of 1786 he was the father of a daughter, Maria. She was born in Bodenstown, where Matilda was forced to live because a serious rift had developed between her and the Witheringtons. Tone heartily disliked his brother-in-law and had simulated a friendship merely to meet Matilda. Edward, perhaps realising this, 'contrived by thousand indirect means to sow feuds and dissensions between us.' Anyway, Tone was on the move again and the security of County Kildare would compensate somewhat for the absence of the husband and father. As part of his necessary legal training, he was required to spend two years in London: he enrolled himself in the Middle Temple in January 1787. (Seven years later, the eighteen-year-old Daniel O'Connell was to do his stint at Lincoln's and Gray's Inns, with a lifestyle notably different from that of the boulevardier Tone.)

Post-war London was more exciting even than Dublin and, with chambers at 4 Hare Court in the Temple, he was in the centre of one of the richest cities in the world – what his near-coeval, the irascible reformer William Cobbett (1762–1835), was to call 'the great wen'. It was an agreeable playground, and Tone found agreeable companions with whom to share it. Law played little part in his life, but a more appropriate source of income showed itself in earnings from writing. With some friends, he devised a novel, called *Belmont Castle,* which was 'intended to ridicule the execrable trash of the circulating libraries' and was later published in Dublin by his friend, Patrick Byrne, in 1790. Tone also earned Grub Street money from reviews. Like many young men of his class and time, he was not very meticulous about sticking to his marriage vows. He admits in the *Memoirs:*

> At the age of twenty-four, with a tolerable figure and address, in an idle and luxurious capital, it will not be supposed I was without adventures with the fair sex . . . I cherish yet with affection the memory of one charming woman to whom I was extremely attached, and I am sure she will remember me with a mutual regard.

In London, too, another fugue struck him. He had been joined in his chambers by his younger brother William, who had been an officer in the army of the East India Company. Tone received a desolate letter from his father, Peter, 'which I afterwards found much exaggerated. In a transport of rage, I determined to enlist as a soldier in the India Company's service . . . ' This considered dereliction of a wife and infant daughter did eventually shame him but, with the passionate determination that often overpowered his cooler judgement, he and William made their way to India House, only to find that no more ships would be sent that year. 'Had it been the month of March instead of September . . . I should most probably at this hour be carrying a brown musket on the coast of Coromandel,' he noted bitterly. One of the spurs to this precipitate action was disappointment at the refusal of the prime minister, William Pitt (1759–1806), to respond to a scheme for the colonisation of Hawaii, 'delivered by my own hand to the porter in Downing Street'.

There was no question about Tone's later dedication to republicanism – but then he was prepared to exploit any means to find a suitable vocation. He probably realised that this would not be in the courts, though when he returned home he applied himself with his usual vigour to rapid study and succeeded in obtaining the necessary formal legal qualifications. He joined the Leinster circuit and found that 'the law grew every day more and more disgustful.' The ideal career lay elsewhere; for a man, however impecunious, of the Protestant elite, the obvious path lay through politics. Political Ireland in the 1790s was a lively place, after more than sixty

years of cryonic suspension. The war in which
the young Tone had wanted to fight the colonists
had indirectly brought about a modicum of
legislative independence for the Irish Parliament.

Towards the end of the 1770s, the country
felt itself undefended against possible invasion,
since the regular troops were all busy in America
and the local militias were inactive. Volunteer
forces were raised locally, the numbers swelling
from 12,000 in the spring of 1779 to 40,000 by
September. The Volunteers, as they came to be
called, tended to be Protestant and middle-
class, with officers generally from the gentry
and aristocracy. By 1782, when the war was
effectively over, they numbered 60,000, and
under the leadership of the Earl of Charlemont
(1728–99), the Earl of Bristol (1730–1803) and
Henry Flood (1732–91) they became aware of
their political power. The great convention at
Dungannon on 15 February 1782 led to legislative independence and the founding of what
later ages called Grattan's Parliament, after
Henry Grattan (1745–1820), who became the
Volunteers' chief spokesman. (English political
expediency, however, may have been as significant

in the repeal of the Declaratory Act as Volunteer pressure.) The movement was less successful in its attempt to institute parliamentary reform: the measures were thrown out by the House of Commons in 1784. Though individual members – notably Bristol and Grattan – were in favour of Catholic emancipation, Flood and Charlemont were strongly against it. More militant reformers, like Napper Tandy (c. 1737–1803) and Thomas Russell (1767–1803), who was Tone's political and moral tutor, believed that the move failed because the Volunteers had not involved the majority Catholic population in their agitation.

In the independent parliament, 234 of the 300 seats were still the personal property of individuals, and Catholics could neither sit in it nor elect members to it. Even Catholic peers were ineligible to sit in the Irish House of Lords. For Tone, who found little to savour in the law – though he earned enough in his first circuit to pay off his debts – some hope of a parliamentary seat (an elected seat, that is; he could not afford to buy his way in by means of a pocket borough) seemed the ideal solution to

his malaise. A kind of Whig opposition existed
and it appeared to the aspiring parliamentarian
that he might be useful to that party. In 1790
two effective pamphlets, the first attacking the
Buckingham administration and the second,
more significantly, asserting that Ireland should
not be bound by any declaration of war by
England, attracted the notice of the Whigs. The
second pamphlet, called *Spanish War* (a conflict
that did not in fact materialise), showed that
Tone was now a mature political pamphleteer
and that his views were becoming too radical for
the Dublin Whigs. Though he was careful not
to reject the kingship of George III, he urged
that Ireland should spurn the idea of being a
satellite and claim its 'rank among the primary
nations of the world'. This was pretty advanced
stuff, and Byrne, Tone's publisher, suppressed
the document.

Tone had by now become friendly with
Russell, an army officer on half-pay who was
already formulating the political principles that
were to be the basis for the foundation of the
United Irishmen. He joined the Tones in a
rented cottage in what was then the resort of

Irishtown. Matilda's health was delicate and at twenty-one she was pregnant for the third time. The grandfather who had provided them with £500 to begin the legal career had died and she was not mentioned in his will. The 'little box of a house' gave them an idyllic long vacation, with lots of leisure for sea-bathing and leisurely discussions about politics and their economic future. The old idea of colonising the Sandwich Islands, as Hawaii was then called, was floated again; no more than a polite reply to the suggestion was given by the Duke of Richmond. And then Russell was called back as an ensign to the sixty-fourth regiment of foot and sent to Belfast.

The news from France excited them as each new intelligence arrived. If Wordsworth found it bliss 'that dawn to be alive', the young men of Ireland found it 'very heaven'. They were dismayed by Edmund Burke's *Reflections on the Revolution in France,* published in 1790 – 'Mr Burke's famous invective', as Tone described it – and elated at the riposte of Thomas Paine (1737–1809), *The Rights of Man*, the first part of which was published the following February.

Russell was soon to find that the Belfast Volunteers were strongly influenced by post-Bastille ideas. The prosperous market town was mainly Presbyterian and they, as nonconformists, also suffered penal restrictions – though nothing as swingeing as those imposed upon Catholics. The Toleration Act (1719) had given them religious freedom but they still had to pay Anglican tithes, and suffered other debarments. These penalties were the main cause of the Ulster emigration to America throughout the century. Full of Enlightenment ideas – and not unaffected by Jacobinism – such men as William Drennan (1754–1820), the Belfast-born obstetrician with an extensive Dublin practice, Samuel Neilson (1761–1803), the rich draper who founded the United Irishmen's paper, the *Northern Star*, in 1792, Henry Joy McCracken (1767–1798), who led the rising in Antrim in 1798, and Samuel McTier, Drennan's brother-in-law, shared the disappointment that Grattan's Parliament was still closed to Dissenters, as the Presbyterians liked to call themselves, and – when they thought of it – 3 million Catholics.

Tone had by now become a 'white-hot

Catholic' – though not in the Confessional sense, of course – and he was convinced that only with their support and by achieving for them the same relief from political penalty would Ireland blossom as a truly independent country. In August 1791 he wrote his best pamphlet – in fact, probably one of the finest ever written in any national cause – *An Argument on Behalf of the Catholics of Ireland*. He signed it 'Northern Whig', as he was entitled to, since he had formulated, at Russell's request, the resolutions for the Bastille Day celebrations in Belfast. (The third of these – that no reform could be just or efficacious which did not include Catholics – was scarcely mentioned.) The final sentence was typical of his optimism:

Let them [men who are sincere for Ireland's prosperity and future elevation] once cry Reform, and the Catholics, and Ireland, is free, independent and happy.

He was careful to establish his credentials as 'a Protestant of the Church of Ireland, as by law established', and this made his protestation as 'a mere lover of justice and a steady detester of tyranny' the more reasonable. He continued to emphasise his fealty to 'the king and his country' but insisted that there could be no liberty for anyone until 'Irishmen of all denominations' combined against the 'boobies and blockheads'. The unindependent state of Ireland was 'the laughing stock of the knaves who plunder us' and the failure of the 'revolution of 1782' was due to the Volunteers refusing to look for help to Catholics – indeed, to having ignored the majority of the people on the island. He heaped scorn on those who believed 'the tales of old nurses, the terrors of our grandams' that would result from Catholic political emancipation (a word that literally means 'release from slavery'), arguing that Catholics, who could have saved their lands by forswearing and did not do so, could now be trusted to keep the terms 'of a work of compact, and like other compacts, subject to stipulations'.

With similar zest – it was clear that he had enjoyed the writing – he demolished the arguments about their popery, Jacobitism, lack of education, unreadiness for political life and possible demands for the restoration of lost lands and, with all the imperative of his Enlightenment views in the surrounding gloom of obscurantism, reminded his Protestant readers of the simple justice of the Catholic case. The pamphlet was a best-seller, with 6,000 copies sold by the spring of 1792. Its authorship was soon public knowledge, and this resulted in an invitation for Mr Hutton to come to Blefescu to attend a very important meeting of northern radicals in October 1791.

It was characteristic of the man that he referred to both friends and adversaries by nicknames in letters and in his journals. His closest friend, Russell, was 'P.P.' (Clerk of this Parish); John Keogh (1740–1817), who was to become an important figure in a reorganised Catholic Committee, was 'Gog', while *his* colleague, Richard McCormick, was the other Biblical enemy of the Kingdom of God, 'Magog'. Neilson was well-named 'the Jacobin', Tandy less appositely 'the Tribune' and Tone himself was 'Mr Hutton', the second syllable indicating the source. Belfast was called after the rival island in *Gulliver's Travels* (1726). It had been intended by its original creator as a satirised France to the equally pigmy Lilliput which was Georgian England. (Swift, though a late discovery for Tone, had become for him, as for so many others, an ancestral, prophetic voice.) Tone's sobriquet was generated by the shared letters and as a subtle compliment to the town whose intellectuals were so imbued with the ideals of *liberté*, *égalité* and *fraternité*.

3

UNITED IRISHMAN
AND CATHOLIC AGENT

Tone's visit to Belfast was a mixture of conviviality and high seriousness, with an element of dismay at the entrenched suspicion of Catholics still to be found among many Dissenters. Tone's journal entry for Sunday 23 October 1791 ends:

> Persuaded myself and P.P. that we were hungry. Went to Donegall Arms and supped on lobsters. Drunk. Very ill-natured to P.P.; P.P. patient. *Mem:* To do so no more. Went to bed. Gulled P.P. with nonsense. Fell asleep.

It is not surprising that the next entry begins, 'Wakened very sick.' The Society of the United Irishmen had been inaugurated on 18 October.

The idea for this organisation had been mooted by Drennan, and Tone's pamphlet had given a great boost to recruitment. The society was to be, in Russell's words, 'a union of Irishmen of every religious persuasion in order to obtain a complete reform of the legislature, founded on the principles of civil, political and religious liberty'. Drennan had thought of calling the society 'the Brotherhood', regarding it as 'a benevolent conspiracy', but the members all accepted Tone's suggestion and the Belfast branch of the United Irishmen was born. As Tone succinctly recalled in the *Memoirs:* 'We formed our club, of which I wrote the declaration . . . ' This declaration had three resolutions, the first about the necessity of countering the weight of English influence, the second urging 'a complete and radical reform of the representation of the people in Parliament' and the third, which was hardest to sell to the mass of the Dissenters:

> That no reform is practicable, efficacious, or just, which shall not include Irishmen of every religious persuasion.

Though Tone's journals were full of under-graduate, even schoolboy humour (*8th* [October 1792] Breakfast, more beefsteak and onions. Go gentle gales. Fragrant and pretty . . .), he could do the grand style, if he'd the call. The fear among Presbyterians of an emancipated Catholic Ireland, which they affected to believe imminent, was brought home to him at a dinner in the house of Samuel McTier on the second-last night of his visit. Dr William Bruce, a Presby-terian clergyman ('an intolerant high priest', in Tone's words) trotted out the old atavistic cant about the establishment of an inquisition, the recovery of lost Catholic lands and the inability of a papist government to enjoy or extend liberty: 'Almost all the company of his opin-ion . . . ' In spite of this, Tone heartily enjoyed this first visit to Blefescu and always looked forward to going again. His journal entry for 27 October has as one of its concluding sentences the following: 'At 1 o'clock, leave Belfast with heavy hearts, having first taken leave of everybody on the road.'

The work, as he knew, was only beginning, and there was the lowering prospect of his having to return to the Leinster circuit to support his growing family. A Dublin club of the United Irishmen was formed eleven days later, on 9 November, with Tandy as secretary. Other notable members were the brothers Henry (1753–98) and John Sheares (1766–98), Thomas Addis Emmet (1764–1827) – the elder brother of Robert (1778–1803) – all from Cork, Whitley Stokes (1763–1845), later Regius professor of medicine and compiler of an early English–Irish dictionary, Hamilton Rowan (1751–1834) and Lord Edward Fitzgerald (1763–98), the twelfth child of the Duke of Leinster. Three significant founder members were John Keogh, Edward Byrne and Richard McCormick, the leading bourgeois Catholics in the city. In such company, Tone, who had neither wealth nor connections and was not physically assertive, ceased to have influence. Yet it was his stirring defence of the club when it was attacked by John Toler (1745–1831), later Earl Norbury – who was notorious for his support of the Act of Union and his buffoonery as a judge – that brought him to the attention of both John Keogh, by then the effective leader of the Catholic Committee, and his implacable enemy, John Fitzgibbon, later Earl of Clare (1749–1802). Through his system of spies, Fitzgibbon had obtained a copy of a covering note that Tone had sent to Russell with his draft resolutions for Bastille Day in Belfast in 1791. In it he had written: 'I have not said one word that looks like a wish for separation, though I give it to you and your friends as my most decided opinion that such an event would be a regeneration of their country.' This was the basis for a continuing campaign against Tone.

Keogh was the leader of a new breed of mercantile Catholics who had lost patience with the rather languid aristocratic members of the Catholic Committee. He had been born in Dublin in the poorest of circumstances but had become rich. He was one of the first to take advantage of the relaxation of the penal prohibition against Catholics owning property, and his mansion at Mount Jerome became the centre of vigorous agitation for Catholic relief. It was he who had appointed Richard Burke, Edmund's only son, as agent and had accompanied him to London to present a petition, in person, to the Commons. This petition had not been successful, largely because of effective and scurrilous lobbying by the Dublin establishment. The 1792 Catholic Relief Bill of Sir Hercules Langrishe (1731–1811) allowed Catholics to practise as solicitors and barristers – one of the beneficiaries was the young Daniel O'Connell – though not to take the silk. It still withheld the franchise from them, however.

It was felt that Burke had failed and, having eased him out with a handshake of £2,000, Keogh offered the job to Tone. Though no great shakes as a public speaker, Tone was clearly effective in print, energetic in pursuit of his ideals and the obvious go-between for Catholics and Dissenters. He was also good company – though perhaps a little lacking in *gravitas* to suit the austere Keogh – and there was no denying his energy or willingness to travel all over the country. Plans were already under way for a convention which would be at once an indication of solidarity and determination and a focus for further agitation. Tone was in Belfast again for the Volunteer celebrations of the third anniversary of *Quatorze Juillet* and returned later with Keogh to investigate the sectarian troubles caused by the Protestant Peep of Day Boys and the reaction of the Catholic Defenders to them. His journal records with characteristic cheeriness:

> Journal of the proceedings of John Hutton, Esq, on his third journey to the North of Ireland; including the artful negotiations with the Peep-of-day-boys and sundry peers of the realm; also, his valorous entry into, and famous retreat out of, the city of Rathfriland; interspersed with sundry delectable adventures and entertaining anecdotes. *Vive le Roi!*

The present 'city of Rathfriland' is a hilltop village just north of the Mourne Mountains in County Down with a population of rather less than 3,000 (and far fewer in Tone's time) but it is typical of Mr Hutton's mock-heroic style that he should have chartered it. He slid in and out of the village in spite of threats of 'houghing' (the hamstringing that both factions practised on rival herds). The Peep of Day Boys were to be the mainstay of the Orange Order, which was founded three years later at Loughgall, County

Armagh. Of greater satisfaction was his dinner in Drogheda with the Catholic bishops of the northern province, 'all very pleasant, sensible men'.

The convention, known jibingly as the Back Lane Parliament, met between 3 and 8 December in Tailors Hall and was an important first step in the politicisation of what had hitherto been regarded as the *canaille*. In fact, the 231 delegates were prosperous merchants and country gentlemen and, of these, 48 were United Irishmen. Clare correctly identified Tone as a man to watch, not so much due to his membership of the club as because of his part in the empowerment of Catholics. He was adamantly opposed to any relief, arguing, with impeccable logic, that a Catholic parliament would soon break the connection with Britain and that this, coming so soon after the loss of the American colonies, might fragment the already great British Empire, which was now effectively ruling Canada and India. Peel was later to use the same logic in his opposition to full emancipation but was more prepared to offer substantial relief to Catholics than was the absolutist Fitzgibbon.

The convention was a success, with a remarkable degree of accord. It drew up a petition requiring 'the total abolition of all distinctions' between Irishmen and agreed that its presentation should be directly to the king, thereby bypassing not only the College Green parliament but even the Westminster one. The British had always tended to be more lenient than the Irish Ascendancy and there was the usual agitation, with grand juries condemning the convention as illegal. Tone, showing a greater degree of legal expertise than he ever admitted to, made the case for the Catholics and had it approved by two eminent lawyers. The delegates went to London via Belfast, where their carriage was drawn by citizens to the docks. They held out to see the king in person and were greeted cordially at their audience on 2 January 1793. It seemed that emancipation was at hand. The climate of opinion was more in their favour than it had been in the previous year. War with France was inevitable, and the last thing that Pitt and his adjutant, Henry Dundas (1742–1811), wanted was a disaffected Ireland. They needed Catholics to man their armies and navies and were prepared for once to overrule the pleas from Dublin. Louis XVI and Marie Antoinette were guillotined on 21 January and war was declared by France shortly afterwards.

The new relief act fell short of expectations. The chief secretary, Robert Hobart, Fourth Earl of Buckingham, proved a much tougher and more skilful negotiator than anybody the convention could supply. At their meeting with him on the day of Louis Capet's execution, he pared down the relief that he was prepared to offer, and the delegation, in disarray, felt bound to accept. The measure became law on 9 April; its reliefs were substantial by the previous year's standards: equal franchise with Protestants, the right to become magistrates, hold service commissions and most public offices, take degrees in Trinity (deferred till March 1794) and carry arms. (The business of representation in Parliament would not be settled for thirty-six years, and by then there was no parliament in College Green.) In return, the agitation must end. Tone blamed Keogh for the collapse and from then on became much more radical in his approach to Irish affairs. The Catholic Committee disintegrated in a flurry of self-rending and mutual recrimination. Tone was again without occupation, but before going out of existence the committee voted him £1,500 and a gold medal. This would tide him and his family, which was now larger by a fourth child, Francis Rawdon – named after Lord Moira, who had arranged the vital meeting with George III at the court of St James – over for a while. Then there seemed no option but the hated practice of the law.

4

THE JACKSON AFFAIR

One of the miserable aspects of the acquiescence by the Catholic Committee was the betrayal, as Tone saw it, of the United Irishmen. They seemed to have settled for Catholic relief and ignored the wider aspects of parliamentary reform which would have benefited the Dissenters. He also disapproved of their agreement to cease agitation forthwith – and not just because the committee's dissolution meant that he no longer had congenial employment. The war with France gave the government in both Britain and Ireland the excuse to take emergency powers to curb anything that was against the national interest; this was interpreted by the Dublin government to include political agitation. The Volunteers were banned in March 1793 and the defence of the country was vested in new county militias. The early conscriptive method of recruitment resulted in rioting and hangings (mainly of Defenders) but a voluntary system soon produced a force of 20,000. The rank and file of the militias was inevitably Catholic, with the exception of those of the north-east and counties such as Donegal and Cork. It was an article of faith with Tone that, in the event of a successful French landing, the militiamen would side with the invaders. In fact, they generally resisted the insurgents when the country rose in 1798.

Tone's wife and family were living at this time in a little cottage in Kildare, on the estate of the Wolfes of Blackhall, where his father had been a freehold tenant. (Tone's two forenames had been chosen by his father in tribute to the squire, Theobald Wolfe.) Though he knew that Fitzgibbon would do his best to injure him both in his legal career and in the political sphere, Tone's credit with the Catholic population was high: he would still have enough briefs from Catholic sources to be able to support his family. He spent the remainder of 1793 in the cottage, which he called 'Chateau Boue', in mock solidarity with the mud cabins of the peasants.

The government, by passing the Convention Act on 16 August, had made sure that there would be no repeat of the great Volunteer convention of 1782, and it began to use its emergency powers to proceed against known members of the United Irishmen. Rowan was arrested in December because of an 'inflammatory' 'Address to the Volunteers of Ireland' published two years earlier and in February 1794 was sentenced to two years in Newgate Jail (which had been built only twenty years before, near where Tone had spent his childhood). It must be said, however, that his incarceration was by modern penological standards relatively civilised: his wife and family visited him daily and he was free to move about the prison. (Drennan was arraigned on the same charge and acquitted; thereafter, he dropped out of politics and became one of the founders of the Belfast Academical Institution in 1814.)

Tone, whose career throughout his life seemed more like that of a cork tossed on the waves than of a well-steered boat, now found himself involved in a spy melodrama with not-unexpected elements of farce. In the early months of 1794, Russell, no longer a justice of the peace in Dungannon – a position he had taken up after selling his commission and being swindled out of the money – accepted the more congenial, if no better paid, post of librarian to the Belfast Reading Society (the nucleus of what was later known as the Linen Hall Library). Tone, sorely missing his closest friend, was staying in Dublin to be able to accept any legal work that might come his way, when he found himself involved in a mishandled mission of espionage.

In April 1794 two rather incompetent conspirators, William Jackson (c. 1737–95) and John Cockayne, arrived in Dublin acting as agents for the French government and took rooms on Dame Street. Jackson was of Irish birth and had taken orders; he had at one time been chaplain to the notorious Duchess of Kingston, whom he had followed into exile to France. It was there that a strong radicalism, initiated by the American War, had made him a confirmed revolutionary. He had confided the nature of his mission to Kingston's attorney, John Cockayne, who had agreed to accompany him. Before they left, Cockayne had won from Pitt the promise of a pension and a waiver of all his debts in exchange for information. To add to the ludicrousness of the scenario, the spies' contact with the United Irishmen was Leonard McNally (1752–1820), who was soon to become the most successful government spy in Irish history (and later the author of the famous ballad 'The Lass of Richmond Hill'). Jackson visited Rowan in Newgate, and it was he who suggested that Tone, as the most proficient word-man, should prepare a document indicating the true state of feeling in Ireland. Tone agreed and wrote the paper on the evening of 14 April, bringing it to Rowan the next morning. It was certainly the document that Jackson wanted, with its concluding asseveration that, of a French invasion force of 10,000, 7,000 could establish a bridgehead in the west and advance into the middle of the country, while the rest could secure Dublin:

> In that event, the North would rise to a man, and so having possession of three-fourths of the country; and the capital,

the remaining part, were it so inclined, could make no resistance.

Tone's attitude to the document was characterised by his usual mixture of efficiency, breeziness and naivety, with a strong dash of wishful thinking. He seemed suddenly to realise in what dangerous waters he was bobbing when he took the piece of writing back from Jackson before he had had a chance to read it and handed it to Rowan, permitting him to make a copy but asking him to burn the original. For all he knew, Jackson might have been a British agent. Rowan in fact worked on the appraisal himself and made several copies of the emended document but did destroy the original, as he had been bid. Tone realised how compromised his own position was: the style was clearly his, and Fitzgibbon and the authorities would immediately recognise the source. The suggestion that he was the ideal person to travel with the appraisal to France, made at a later meeting, he had to dismiss. A document signed by Tone on 3 May 1794 and given in full in the part of the *Memoirs* written by his son William reports that:

I then added that with regard to my going to France, I was a man of no fortune, that my sole dependence was on a profession; that I had a wife and three children, whom I dearly loved, solely depending on me for support; that I could not go and leave them totally unprovided for, and trusting to the mercy of providence for existence; and that consequently, with regard to me, the going to France was a thing totally impossible. They all agreed that what I said was reasonable, but there *was no offer of money or pecuniary assistance of any kind held out to induce me to change my determination.*

In this matter, as in so much else in his life, one gets the impression that Tone allowed chance and circumstance to determine his course. His usual position was somewhere between an innocent opportunism where his career was concerned and an adventurous sense of life's possibilities. Under better circumstances, a journey to France as a kind of ambassador for the United Irishmen would have pleased him greatly; to put it perhaps crudely, he would have enjoyed the *craic,* and when his French adventure came to fruition on 1 February 1796, he threw himself into the task with his usual enthusiasm, but – and it is a significant 'but' – in the interim he had lived for five months in America and had nearly become a New Jersey farmer.

One reason for his reluctance to leave was that the Catholic Committee had not delivered the promised £1,500 – though when Jackson was arrested on 28 April on a charge of high treason, Tone was sorely tempted to follow Rowan, who escaped from Newgate three days later and made his way to France. The appraisal document signed by Rowan had been found among Jackson's papers, but there was nothing to connect him with conspiracy except Cockayne's rather weak evidence that Tone had been with him in Jackson and Rowan's company. Though both Fitzgibbon and Westmorland would have been pleased to make an example of Tone, they decided to wait and use Rowan's departure as an excuse to ban the United Irishmen. What had been a legal, reforming association was driven underground and became rather more radical. Tone was allowed, in an arrangement made by a friend in high places, to provide a statement of limited involvement in the organisation and a promise to leave the country with his family.

He spent the rest of the year at Chateau Boue but rather unwisely returned to Dublin in December to be employed again by the Catholic Committee. The political situation changed dramatically on 4 January 1795 with the appointment of the liberal Earl Fitzwilliam as Lord Lieutenant. As usual, the situation in Ireland was dictated by political exigency in London: Pitt needed Whig support to maintain his war coalition. Fitzwilliam, who was in favour of Catholic Emancipation, used his brief period in high office to dismiss many of the anti-reform Dublin Castle officials and encouraged Grattan to introduce a new Catholic relief bill on 12 February. Like other reformers before and since, he moved too fast, alienated many who had the ear of prominent Tories and was recalled on 23 February. The way was free for the reinstated officials to proceed with their clampdown on any form of relief. Jackson's trial began on 23 April and one week later, on the day he was due for sentencing, he was found slumped in the dock, dead from poison that his wife had smuggled in.

Tone's name had been mentioned many times during the trial and he realised that it was time for him to leave the country, taking his wife and children with him. The writing had been on the wall since Fitzwilliam's recall, and the intelligence from Russell in Belfast was that the United Irishmen had reformed themselves into a revolutionary society. The Catholic Committee lived up to its promise and Tone was able to pay off his debts and retain £796 as finance for his exodus. He took with him Matilda, the couple's three surviving children and their uncle Arthur and aunt Mary. Their port of embarkation was Belfast, which the party reached on 21 May, and the three weeks before the sailing – on the *Cincinnatus,* bound for Wilmington, Delaware – were spent renewing old acquaintances and planning new strategies. Before leaving Dublin, Tone had indicated to Russell and Emmet that America might be no more than a staging-post on the way to France. Certainly, when he climbed Cave Hill with Russell, Neilson and McCracken to the highest point, McArt's Fort (known to later generations as 'Napoleon's nose' because of the supposed resemblance of the hill's crest to the profile of *l'empereur*), the oath they took was as near a commitment to armed action as it could be without actually stating it. The men vowed:

> never to desist in our efforts until we had subverted the authority of England over our country and asserted our independence.

The Tones' voyage on the *Cincinnatus* began on 13 June and the Delaware River was reached on 1 August. The party lived for six weeks in a cabin eight feet by six; they had plenty of provisions, supplied by Belfast friends, and a useful medical chest provided by Dr Mac-Donnell. Scarcity of fresh water was their greatest privation and Tone – as ever, rising to a challenge – appointed himself physician to the 300 or so emigrants who had to put up with even more cramped conditions. A week from landfall, they were boarded by a recruiting party from three British frigates who press-ganged many of the deckhands and some of the passengers. Tone himself was seized and might have had a different fate altogether but for the persistent screams of his wife and sister. (The Royal Navy's habit of boarding even neutral ships was to be one of the causes of the war with America in 1812.)

The family found lodgings in Philadelphia but Tone's plans to hasten to France received a setback when the French minister Adet did not seem anxious to help him, in spite of a strong recommendation from Rowan, who had left France after the fall of Robespierre in July. Tone had little enthusiasm for settling in Pennsylvania, disliking the German-Americans he met there and finding the land of the free and the home of the brave strangely like Britain in its materialism and lack of republican virtues. Yet there seemed no alternative to settling, and negotiations about the purchase of a farm near Princeton, New Jersey, were well advanced when letters arrived from Keogh, Russell and the Simms brothers – the Belfast tanners who were still United Irishmen, in spite of the government's ban and great changes in Ulster. They all urged Tone to try to get to France and persuade the Directory that the time was ripe for invasion. William Simms proposed to him a loan of up to £200 and a now-more-enthusiastic Adet offered to pay for the passage and provide him with letters of introduction. The letters were gladly accepted but Tone paid his own way, leaving New York on 1 January 1796 on the *Jersey* and landing at Le Havre just a month later, after an unusually stormy voyage.

5

BANTRY BAY

Of all Tone's achievements, none was more impressive than his success in persuading the Directory to assemble a fleet of forty-five ships and nearly 15,000 men for the purpose of invading Ireland. The placing of the expedition in the charge of Lazare Hoche (1768–97), who was, after Napoleon, the leading French soldier of the age – and, unlike the latter (who never held lowly rank, in spite of his famous sobriquet) was promoted in one leap from corporal to general – was an indication of the importance with which the government regarded it. Tone himself was breveted *chef de brigade* in the French army, as both an honour and, he hoped, insurance against the unspeakable savagery of a traitor's death, should he be captured. It was a remarkable piece of persuasion by a man with little money, few contacts, practically no French and only a letter in cipher from Adet as credentials, and it took a weary eleven months to achieve results. This delay was a comment on the prevailing political situation: egalitarianism has many virtues but by definition it lacks the hierarchical structure and chain of command that achieves expedition of orders.

'James Smith', a gentleman from the United States, arrived in Paris on 12 February and set to work at once. The deliberate lack of originality of the assumed name, like the earlier 'Mr Hutton', was typical. France, especially the northern departments, was full of English agents, and Tone knew that a *nom de guerre* would be easily penetrable. He was not terribly concerned about concealment, feeling that making himself known, rather than security, was the priority. One of his early calls was upon the American ambassador, James Monroe (1758–1831), who was to serve two consecutive terms as president (1816–24) and formulate the 'Monroe Doctrine', which rendered the Americas, North and South, secure from further Old World colonisation. Tone was directed to the Ministry of Foreign Affairs, where he was introduced to Charles Delacroix, perhaps the father of the great colourist, who passed him on to Nicholas Madgett, the Irishman who had sent Jackson on his ill-fated mission to Ireland.

It became clear that, although the government approved the idea of attacking England through Ireland – especially when Tone assured them of Catholic and Dissenter support – the tactical difficulty was the disorganised state of the navy. The armies of the Revolution had done well: Hoche himself had driven the Austrians out of Alsace and ended the Vendée civil war, and that year Napoleon was to demonstrate his military genius by subduing Italy. The navy was different: it needed seasoned officers with technical skills – which essentially meant aristocrats, who could not be sure of obedience from the fo'c'sle. The superiority of Britannia's wave-ruling fleet was well known: the blockade it maintained had crippled France's economy; Tone found his pounds were very strong against the franc. Any invasion fleet had to slip the ships riding west of Brest. Yet even if the corruption-ridden Directory diminished the efficiency of the war effort (and led eventually to the extremely aristocratic rule of *l'empereur)*, the Royal Navy had its own internal battles to fight against the aristocratic and venal Admiralty.

Tone overcame the *longueurs* of the ante-rooms in which he passed much of his time by nightly visits to the theatre and the opera, but he was lonely, missing his family and friends like Russell, with whom the sojourn in France would have meant even more *craic* than old Belfast days. St Patrick's Day found Tone dining 'alone in the Champs Élysées. Sad! Sad!' and the journal entry for 18 March reads: 'Blank! Theatre in the evening.' His most successful ploy was to bypass all intermediaries and speak directly to Lazare Carnot (1753–1823), whose military past and unimpeachable reputation had made him the significant voice of the Directory. On 24 February Tone had marched into the Luxem-bourg Palace, hiding his extreme nervousness, and demanded to see the then most powerful man in France. The meeting went well: as he put it, 'I think I came off very clean.' Indeed, he was eventually successful in the lobbying, though time and again his hopes were dashed.

The granting of the army commission on 19 June – which was not in fact signed until 18 July – gave him sufficient money to support himself, and he found in Hoche, appointed on 12 July to lead the expedition, a fellow spirit.

Tone's period of pleading had happily co-incided with Directory plans for some kind of invasion of England, perhaps through the Bristol Channel – though Hoche had consistently advocated Ireland as the place to fight the English. Tone's advocacy to Carnot of an Irish landing played a significant part in having the other members of the Directory agree, in principle, to the Irish venture. French intelligence confirmed Tone's appraisal of the situation, and strong urging by his fellow Irishmen Lord Edward Fitzgerald and Arthur O'Connor (1763–1852), who was then in Hamburg to lobby Hoche, finally won agreement. Various points of landing were considered, including Galway Bay and Lough Swilly in Donegal, but by the time the fleet was assembled and ready to sail from Brest on 15 December, the destination had been changed to Bantry Bay or, should that fail, the estuary of the Shannon. The change was dictated by the lateness of the season, Bantry Bay's nearness to France and the fear that British intelligence had learned of their earlier plan.

The five-month delay has been blamed upon the concomitant disarray of the navy, but the reluctance, inevitable in the uneasy years after the Terror, of senior officers to be associated with a risky enterprise was also a factor. Eventually a cadre was formed and a huge fleet was marshalled at Brest. It consisted of eighteen ships of the line (the largest men-o'-war able to hold their places in the line of battle), thirteen frigates (warships second in rank to the line ships), six corvettes (ships with a single bank of cannon), and so on down to the small, fast luggers which were used for conveying messages from ship to ship when out of range of semaphore. There were forty-three vessels in all, and they carried a force of 14,750 soldiers – a veritable Armada. Ironically, it proved as ineffective as the sixteenth-century Spanish attempt, and for much the same reasons: bad luck, inferior seamanship and, most of all, the appalling weather. As the commemorative medallion struck in 1588 had it: *Flavit Jehovah et dissipati sunt*. ('Jehovah blew and they were scattered.') The French fleet were scattered as effectively as the ships of Medina Sidonia (though they did not meet the same fate as the hapless Armada) and by Christmas Day it was clear that the adventure had failed. Tone's entry in his journal for 26 December sums up the débâcle sadly and also shows the essential ebullience of the writer:

> Well, England has not had such an escape since the Spanish Armada, and that expedition, like ours, was defeated by weather; the elements fight against us, and courage is here of no avail. Well, let me think no more about it; it is lost and let it go! I am now a Frenchman, and must regulate my future plans accordingly.

Misfortune had dogged them from the beginning. There were three exit channels from the haven of Brest: the Iroise, the safest and the one normally used, would, the commanders felt, take them straight into the range of the British squadron under the brilliant Edward Pellew; the

Canal de Four, the northern gut, would have given away the French fleet's destination; so they attempted to file through the dangerous, narrow Raz de Sein. Almost immediately, the *Seduisant*, one of the ships of the line, struck a rock and sank with only 45 of the complement of 1,300 aboard being saved. Seventeen other vessels, including the *Indomitable* (with Tone on board), made the passage safely; the rest followed the change of orders (a continuing feature of the expedition) and sailed through the Iroise. One of the last to leave was the *Fraternité*, with Hoche on board. She was soon lost in a fog and then blown out into the Atlantic; she never caught sight of the main fleet until she reappeared at La Rochelle on 14 January. Since she carried much of the money and supplies for the invading army – and the propaganda material upon which Tone had laboured so effectively – it meant that the expedition was literally without its head.

The Marquis de Grouchy (1766–1847), an aristocrat who had sided with the people at the beginning of the Revolution, took command and might have been prepared to risk a landing with his 6,000 men at Bantry, which they had reached by 21 December, but the easterly storms, which grew more vehement each day, prevented his fleet from entering the bay. Riding the storm out so close to the coast was impossible. Slipped anchors and severed cables, the hard handling of the clumsy ships, difficulties with inter-ship communication and general confusion about procedure meant that by 27 December, all ships that could be contacted were ordered back to Brest. Tone's remark recorded in his diary entry for 21 December has been remembered ever since as an example of his frustration: 'we were near enough to toss a biscuit ashore'. If Hoche had been able to beat the contrary winds and join up with the third of the fleet that had reached Bantry, he might well have landed with some sort of force and perhaps have captured the virtually undefended Cork. If the unusual easterlies that had brought the fleet to the Irish coast so quickly had reverted to the accustomed south-west airflow, even at gale strength, a fair proportion of the scattered force could have made the passage into the safe waters of the bay and perhaps changed the course of history.

The remarkable thing was that, once they

had cleared the guardian isle of Ushant, they met no British ship either going or returning. French confusion was matched by Admiralty disdain and a low opinion of Johnny Frenchman, who could not possibly be considering an invasion in the bleak midwinter, even in the unlikely event of the Directory's having the resources for such an action, the British thought. The planned destination was not known to most of the French masters until their orders were opened at sea. This ignorance was shared by the Irish who were supposed to rise: Munster remained quiet, leaderless and unaware of the tantalising proximity of the invasion fleet. When the authorities realised by what a hair's breadth disaster had been accidentally avoided, they did what they could throughout 1797 to prevent any likelihood of a rising.

The anti-Defender Insurrection Act, passed on 24 March 1796, had given the military power to impose curfews, engage in arms searches and disregard habeas corpus. Oath-taking and administering were made capital offences. General Gerard Lake (1744–1808) imposed martial law on Ulster on 13 March and effectively disarmed all those 'not serving the Crown'. (Significantly, he reviewed Orange marches in Lisburn and Lurgan on 12 July.) Many outlawed United Irishmen, including Neilson, Russell and Mc-Cracken, remained in prison, and William Orr (1766–97), a moderate Antrim farmer ('our murdered brother', as Drennan described him in the famous ballad), was hanged at Carrickfergus on the charge of 'administering' on 14 October. Lake's measures of disarming Catholic and Dissenter and publicly approving the yeomanry now seems a deliberate policy of incitement: local insurrection without French support could easily be suppressed and no one would question the methods.

Tone, now an adjutant general of the Armée de Sambre et Meuse, was involved in a further attempt at invasion: on 8 July he boarded the appropriately named *Vrijheid* ('Freedom'), the flagship of the Dutch fleet which was ready to sail from Texel, the most westerly of the Frisian Islands. As if on cue, the favourable winds changed, and the fleet was unable to sail. The inevitable disagreements between General Daendels and Admiral de Winter, the army and navy commanders, broke out and that expedition was abandoned. Daendels immediately conceived a new plan that involved an Irish landing via the western ports of Scotland, and Tone was dispatched to Hoche's headquarters in Wetzlar to ask him to command it. Hoche, now terminally ill with tuberculosis, was manifestly unfit even to walk and died on 19 September aged twenty-nine. When the Dutch fleet sailed, three weeks later, it was almost wiped out by Admiral Duncan's English fleet at Camperdown. Tone's innate cheerfulness and a remarkable belief in his invincibility caused him to write in a late comment on 23 December:

> It was well I was not on board the *Vryheid*. If I had it would have been a pretty piece of business. I fancy I am not to be caught at sea by the English: for this is the second escape I have had, and by land I mock myself of them.

6

'SO BAD AN ANATOMIST'

Tone's sorrow at Hoche's death and the failure of any help he had hoped to give the sorely tried United Irishmen and Defenders was somewhat mitigated by his reunion with Matilda and the children, who had moved from Hamburg to Paris. His journal records some of the pleasure of that short and precious time: 'April 27 to May 17: Having obtained leave of absence for two decades [sic], I have spent the last twenty days deliciously with my family, at Paris', but later entries show his sense of failure, as in that for 26 May: 'My blood is cooling fast. "My May of life is falling to the sear, the yellow leaf." It would be singular if, after all, I were to go out to India.' It was typical that, even in extremity, he could not resist punning on Macbeth's bleak words.

By now, internal revolutionary Directory politics

had led to the purge of Fructidor in September, caused Carnot to flee the country as a 'royalist', cast suspicion on all involved in his ventures, including Tone, and allowed the Corsican artillery genius to begin his rise to power. Napoleon had little interest in an attack on England through Ireland, preferring to build up the navy until it might control La Manche and then invade Kent by the shortest possible sea route. He was polite but non-committal when Tone urged a landing to give heart to those who were about to rise at home. Napoleon was more interested in Egypt and a possible landing in India, and in fact all the scattered Irish insurrections were easily quenched because, except for Humbert's gallant, if minuscule, force, the indispensable French were never really 'on the say', and the expected – and sorely needed – reinforcement of Hardy's 3,000 men never arrived.

Tone spent the summer in Paris, raging with frustration and grief at the news of the failure of each of the attempts of his friends at establishing the Irish Republic. He was conscious of a sense of non-fulfilment of promises, amounting in depressed moments to betrayal. This was somewhat ironic, as history shows, since government spies and paid informers were successful as never before or since and had fully briefed the authorities in Dublin about plans and personnel. Lord Edward Fitzgerald had died from wounds suffered during his arrest; many other friends, including McCracken, Henry Munro (1758–98), and even Tone's brother Matthew, had been hanged. There was, then, a kind of fatalism about Tone's sailing on 16 September from Brest in the *Hoche,* the flagship of a small invasion fleet carrying with them 3,000 troops led by Admiral Bompard. The insurrection was over and the participants were paying the price: 30,000 people had died – the lucky ones in battle, the others choked to death by the hangman or subject to the cruelty of the pitch-cap. The country was at the mercy of freebooting 'loyalists', whose terror was winked at by the military authorities. Yet Tone felt that, as a founder of the United Irishmen and someone who had played at least some part in the urging of a rising, he felt bound to return: he had wound the clock and must hear it strike.

The invasion force was met by a British squadron off the north coast of Donegal on 10 October. Bompard advised Tone to transfer to the schooner, which could outsail the enemy ships, warning him that, whereas they would be prisoners of war, he, whose presence with the fleet was already known, thanks to the English spy network in Brest, would certainly be hanged. He refused and distinguished himself as a gunnery officer during the uneven battle. Continuing gales as ever provided the stage directions to his drama; it was not until 31 October that he was brought ashore in leg-irons at Buncrana. He recognised among the reception party an old undergraduate acquaintance of his, Sir George Hill, whom he greeted 'with as much sang-froid as you might expect from his character', as that worthy recalled, and who, as MP for Derry and a loyalist officer in both the militia and yeomanry, was now the diametrical opposite of his prisoner.

Tone was taken to Derry Jail in leg-irons – but still wearing the colourful uniform of a French colonel – and thence to the Provost Prison in the Royal Barracks at Dublin Castle, reaching the capital on 8 November. His trial two days later was a court martial at which he admitted the charge of acting against the government of George III but, in a permitted statement, insisted that his actions were intended to bring about the separation of the two countries: 'From my earliest youth I have regarded the connection between Ireland and Great Britain as the curse of the Irish nation.' This was why he had enlisted in the French army, why he risked disaster to his wife and children and why he was now ready 'at this day to add the sacrifice of my life.' He had a request to make: 'I ask that the court should adjudge me the death of a soldier, and let me be shot by a platoon of grenadiers.' This request was made 'in consideration of the uniform which I wear . . . ' The request was not granted and Lord Cornwallis, the Lord Lieutenant, insisted that the court martial's sentence of hanging be carried out on 12 November. (Cornwallis did, however, direct that the other part of the court's order – the severing and exposure in a public place of his head – be waived.)

Some of Tone's friends from Trinity and the Irish bar, including John Philpot Curran (1750–1817), tried for a stay of execution, arguing that, since Tone was not a British officer, a British military court had no power to try him. A stay was granted, but by then Tone lay near death with a self-inflicted wound. On the morning fixed for his execution, he had cut his throat, injuring the windpipe but missing the jugular vein. Later, when he heard he might yet survive, he remarked in French to Lentaigne, the émigré surgeon who attended him so conscientiously, 'I am sorry I have been so bad an anatomist.' He lingered until 19 November, dying probably of septicaemia from the infected wound. He was thirty-five years old. He took some consolation from the fact that his wife and family were being cared for by Thomas Wilson, a Scottish radical, who married Matilda in 1816. Tone's body was taken to the house where his parents were lodging and buried on 21 November 1798 in the family plot at Bodenstown, the 'green grave' afterwards celebrated by Thomas Davis (1814–45) in his poem for the *Nation*.

Tone was an obvious icon for the Young Irelanders, and the *Memoirs*, edited and extended by his son William and published in 1826, supplied appropriate material for Davis's agenda of the recovering of a cultural and political Irish nationalism that would be more vital than O'Connell's more measured and – as it seemed to the young Turks – more toadying approach. Bodenstown had not till then been a place of pilgrimage. When Davis wrote his poem, the grave was derelict: 'Small shelter, I ween, are the ruined walls there.' Eighty years later, Padraic Pearse found in Tone the appropriate sanction for 'this road before me' and 'the deed that I see/ And the death I shall die.' It was at Bodenstown in 1913, at a celebration of the 150th anniversary of his birth, that Pearse proposed Tone's formal statement of intent 1796, in the Jackson document – 'To break the connection with England, the never-failing source of all our political evils' – as the fundamental tenet of the IRB's revolutionary doctrine.

Not unexpectedly, the enamelling and varnishing of the medallion tended to obscure the man underneath, but then, iconisation is inherently selective. Later Irish leaders, Davis and Pearse among them, have had to succumb to the process of nationalist canonisation. Even Parnell has attained iconhood, for rhetorical purposes, though in his case there was rather more grouting and rendering to be done before the patina was crack-free. When one considers Tone's career and beliefs, as adumbrated at different periods of his short life, he seems an unlikely figure to have become a nationalist and republican icon. If any of the numerous career possibilities that he considered had been successful he might have become vice-governor of the British colony of Hawaii; a rather enlightened captain in General Burgoyne's army (agreeable company for the general if he was anything like the character portrayed in Shaw's *The Devil's Disciple)* and later, perhaps, a colonel in his garrison in Ireland in 1783; an Indian nabob, like Jos Sedley in Thackeray's *Vanity Fair;* a gallant constitutional supporter of Grattan as they tried to defeat the Act of Union in 1800; a New Jersey farmer who might have fought the British with extra zeal in the War of 1812; or one of Napoleon's wittier officers at Austerlitz.

His republicanism, indeed his separatism, was of his time – and was vastly different from that of Davis or Pearse (whose definition of the term was neither that of the merry agnostic Jacobin nor that of the prodigious Anglican balladeer). He was a member – if at the lower levels – of the Protestant Ascendancy and knew little of the 3 million Catholics whose cause he so volubly advanced. Unlike Davis, he had no knowledge at all of the hidden Ireland of the twilit Gaelic culture. The republic he imagined was as unegalitarian as the kingdom that, as an instinctive royalist, he eventually and reluctantly rejected. Throughout his often headlong course, his mien seemed a combination of inert fatalism and hectic opportunism. Yet his writings, which give such a colourful picture of the times, are perennially entertaining, and he emerges as a delightful, self-critical, if self-forgiving, *homme moyen sensuel.* The greatest factors that disqualify him from being seen as a radical exemplar are his cheeriness, inexhaustible humour and aware-ness of besetting faults – qualities almost invariably lacking in your sombre revolutionary. Like Hoche, Russell, McCracken and other friends, he died young, and worthily takes his honoured place among those who tried romantic-ally to sweeten Ireland's wrong in a dark time. Perhaps Thomas Davis, who began his cult, should have the last, rather simplistic, word:

> *For in him the heart of a woman combined*
> *With a heroic life, and a governing mind –*
> *A martyr for Ireland.*

SELECT BIBLIOGRAPHY

Bartlett, T. *Theobald Wolfe Tone*. Dublin, 1997.

Boylan, H. *Wolfe Tone*. Dublin, 1981.

——————. *A Dictionary of Irish Biography*. (3rd ed.) Dublin, 1998.

Connolly, S. J. *The Oxford Companion to Irish History*. Oxford, 1998.

Doherty, J. E. & Hickey, D. J. *A Chronology of Irish History since 1500*. Dublin, 1989.

Elliott, M. *Wolfe Tone: Prophet of Irish Independence*. New Haven, 1989.

Killen, J. *A History of the Linen Hall Library*. Belfast, 1990.

Newmann, K. *Dictionary of Ulster Biography*. Belfast, 1993

Tone, T. W. *Life of Theobald Wolfe Tone: Memoirs, Journals and Political Writings, Compiled and Arranged by William T. W. Tone, 1826* (ed. Bartlett, T.). Dublin, 1998.

Wall, M. *Catholic Ireland in the Eighteenth Century: Collected Essays* (ed. O'Brien, G.). Dublin, 1989.